Cosmo's
Naughty
Notes

Surprise your guy with them!

100 Sexy Stickies
To Tease, Tantalize, and Turn On Your Man

From the Editors of COSMOPOLITAN

Welcome to *Cosmo's* Naughty Notes!

This little book is jam-packed with 100 sexy stickies specially designed to delight, surprise, and seduce any man. Whether you use them to pay him a carnal compliment, reveal a taboo fantasy, or suggest a randy rendezvous, these notes are a surefire way to ignite his passion. You can also make your next special occasion sizzle with red-hot wishes for his birthday, Valentine's Day, the Fourth of July, and more. Plus, you'll find blank stickies in the back so that you can write your very own naughty notes—for his eyes only, of course. All you do is peel off a note and leave it on his pillow, dashboard, bathroom mirror, or wherever he might find it....Then watch his temperature rise!

—The Editors of *Cosmopolitan*

I won't bite...
unless you
beg for it.

You've been
a very
bad boy.
It's time
for a
spanking.

I don't
plan to get
out of bed
all weekend.

DO
NOT
DISTURB!

Care to
join me?

Your To-Do List for Today

- [ ] **Laundry**
- [ ] **Grocery store**
- [ ] **Buy bottle of wine**
- [ ] **Me**

Know what
I could use
right now?

Your lips
on mine.

XOXOXO

During your lunch hour, you can spend 20 minutes enjoying a sandwich or 20 minutes enjoying me.

Did I ever
tell you
I was voted
most flexible
in my
yoga class?

CARNAL COUPON

Entitles

_____

to one
lay-there-and-love-it
sack session

CARNAL COUPON

CARNAL COUPON

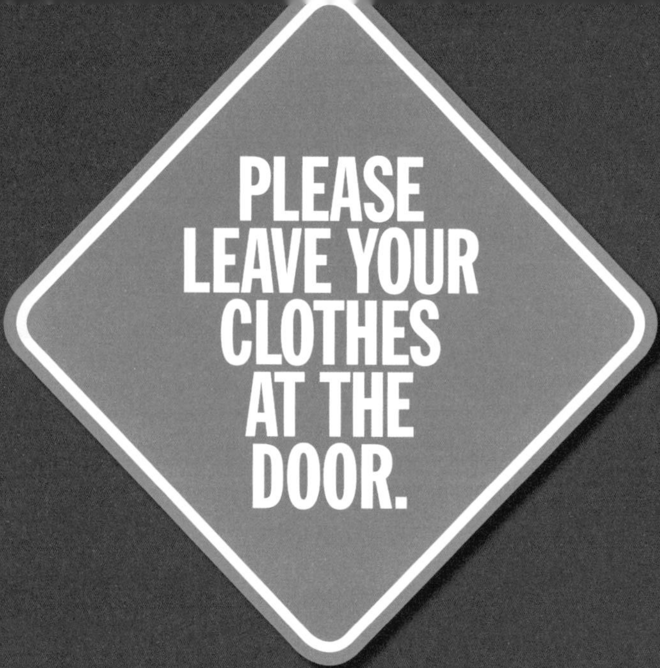
PLEASE
LEAVE YOUR
CLOTHES
AT THE
DOOR.

I'm in need
of some
stress relief.

Got any ideas?

XOXOXO

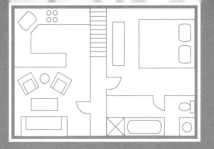

Mark your favorite spot in the house to have sex. Then count to thirty. I'll meet you there.

...TO LEAVE
THE LIGHTS ON.
I WANT TO
SEE EVERYTHING.

Since we're going to visit my family, I have to warn you: The sight of my twin bed makes me want to do things that would shock my parents.

Some guys turn heads.
You inspire 360-degree gawking.

Take your pick:

- ☐ Long kiss
- ☐ Deep kiss
- ☐ Wet kiss
- ☐ All of the above

Thanks for
last night...

and tonight.

See you later.

XOXOXO

I'd bend over backward for you. Can I prove it later tonight?

Please
hand over
your jeans.
I'll return them
to you in an
hour...or however
long it takes
to blow
your mind.

I had a dream about you last night.

Turns out, I have a wild imagination.

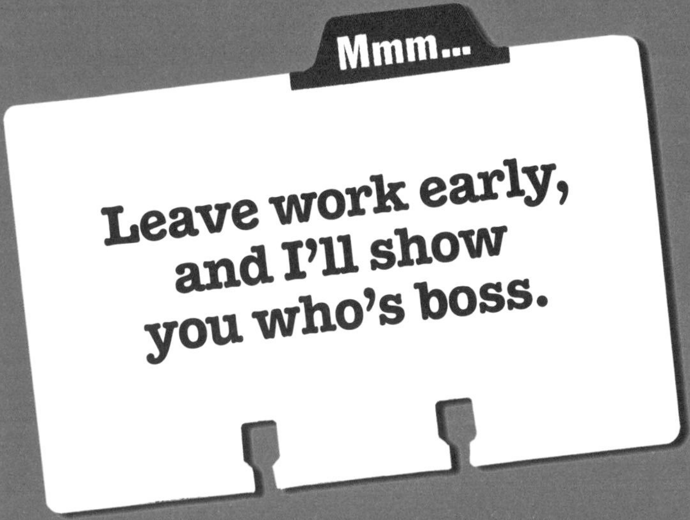
Mmm...
Leave work early, and I'll show you who's boss.

**GUARANTEES
EXCLUSIVE
EROTIC
ENTRY
TO A
VERY
HOT
SPOT.**

I'm rereading all the classics.

THE COSMO KAMA SUTRA

99 mind-blowing sex positions

The Editors of COSMOPOLITAN

Tonight I plan to tackle *The Cosmo Kama Sutra.*

A FEW OF

_____'S

FAVORITE THINGS:

- ☑ Your face
- ☑ Your lips
- ☑ Your eyes
- ☑ Your_____

The Guinness Book called. They said your stamina is record breaking.

To: _____

For your birthday,
I've decided to
grant you that one
frisky wish you've
been begging for.

Love: _____

Call your roommate and tell him you won't be coming home tonight.

XOXOXO

Grab the
check and
skip dessert,
because I have
something better
waiting for
you at home.

I'm dying
to take
another trip
south of
your border.

Let's make this a red-hot holiday season!

This
bad girl
deserves a
spanking.

This Fourth
of July, you're
going to see
lots of fireworks.

Then we'll
go see the
ones outside.

If my friends knew how good you are, they'd beg me to share.

XOXOXO

Meet me
in the
shower....

I'm feeling
dirty.

Let's do a blind taste test:

I'll hide a dab

of honey

on my body

and you

have to use

your tongue

to find it.

I DARE YOU...

...TO DOWNLOAD A NAUGHTY MOVIE AND REENACT A STEAMY SCENE WITH ME.

CARNAL COUPON

Entitles

to one mind-blowing oral sex session

CARNAL COUPON

CARNAL COUPON

CARNAL COUPON

Stressed?
I know just the
massage oil
that will rub
that out.

You know
that girl who
dumped you?
I'm thinking of
writing her a
thank-you note.

XOXOXO

Before you pick up that new iPhone, let's tire out the camera on your last one.

(We can delete the "evidence" later.)

Let's make this vacation so hot,

we won't be able to show anyone our photos.

I'm so wound up.
Would you mind
meeting me
in the bedroom
to work out
some kinks?

One
New Year's
resolution
I need you to
help me keep:
taking our
sex life to the
next level.

It's laundry night....Know what that means? I'm not wearing any undies.

XOXOXO

If you like

how I look

with my

clothes on,

just wait

until you

see me naked.

Come here, I'll kiss it and make it better.
Everywhere.

Oh Yeah!

Congrats on your promotion!

Now it's my turn to give you a raise!

I just bought the sexiest new lingerie. Meet me in the bedroom for a fashion show.

Bring the whipped cream.

Dessert is on me tonight.

I'm thinking about you right now. Hope I'm not near any mind readers.

XOXOXO

...TO WAKE
UP THE
NEIGHBORS.

Why talk when there are so many other fun other fun ways to use our mouths?

Take your pick:

- [ ] Your place
- [ ] My place
- [ ] A public place

I'M ON A HIGH
C.A.R.B. DIET:

CRAVING

A

RIPPED

BOD

INDULGE ME?

Right now,
as you're
reading this,
I'm thinking
about being
in bed with you.

XOXOXO

Want a
quick break
from watching
the game?
I'll give you a
halftime show
you'll never
forget.

Pretend it's your birthday tonight,

because I have a gift you won't be able to wait another day for.

Think the
sex is good
now? Well,
guess what...
it only gets
better.

NO SHIRT.
NO SHOES.
FULL SERVICE!

I skipped the gym today. Any ideas how I can work up a sweat?

XOXOXO

You may want to soundproof your walls...

'cause I make a lot of noise.

Studies show that the more **below-the-belt pleasure** I give you, the better you'll perform at work.

Let's test it out.

JUST *read* **this** **month's**

We **HAVE** **HOMEWORK** **!**

I'm going through some old Halloween costumes. Wanna help me decide which ones to keep?

Don't do
much at the
gym....

Save energy
for later.

xoxoxo

It's your call: black lace panties or nothing at all?

I know you're in a bad mood.

Let me take off your boxers, and I promise you'll feel 10 times better.

CARNAL COUPON

Entitles _____ to one lusty lap dance

CARNAL COUPON

CARNAL COUPON

CARNAL COUPON

They say
absence makes
the heart
grow fonder.
Does it
make other
things grow
too?

I found
my old
cheerleading
uniform.

It still fits.

GIVE ME AN
OOOOH!

You know what
I'm thankful
for this year?
Having your
body as my
own personal
playground.
XOXOXO

Fantasies are nice.

Reality is better.

Free tonight?

Just one more
reason to
get over that cold:
a night of wild,
wake-the-neighbors
sex with me.

I'd like to
borrow your
mouth for the
entire day.
Hope you can
handle it.

I think you need a new position at work:

OFFICE USE ONLY!

doggie-style, with me over your desk.

I've yet to meet a man who can keep up with me. No pressure.

If I'd known
you were
this good, I
wouldn't have
waited until
the third date.

XOXOXO

You spoil
me rotten.

I like that
in a man.

...TO MAKE
MY TOES CURL...

TWICE IN
A ROW.

YOU
+
ME
-
CLOTHES
=
A LOT
OF FUN!

Fill in the blanks:

"I love it when you start touching me _____,

then move down to my _____,

then finish off by licking my _____."

☑

☐ **Blindfold**

☐ **Handcuffs**

☐ **Paddle**

**(Pick your prop, and
I'll take care of the rest.)**

I don't
know how to
thank you,
so I'll stick with
the standby:
sex so good
you won't
know what
hit you.

I feel kind of
sorry for all those
other guys out
there.
You're just so
much hotter.

XOXOXO

Send Cut Copy Paste Undo

To:

Subject:

Tell your boss that you have to leave early today, then meet me at my place.

Be my sex slave for the next hour. You must fulfill every risqué request.

If you were any yummier, I'd never look at chocolate again.

Let's leave the windows open tonight. No one in our neighborhood will want to miss this show.

Clearly,
you have an
oral fixation.
Don't even
think about
trying to
correct that.

Some girls are
too sweet to
speak up in bed.

I'm not one
of them.

XOXOXO

Ever thought of installing a mirror on your bedroom ceiling? Maybe you should.

Forget the mile-high
club. Next time
we board a
plane, you're
mine before we
leave the gate.

_____

_____

_____

_____

_____

_____

_____

_____

_____

_____

_____

_____

COSMOPOLITAN

Edited by John Searles
Book Design by Peter Perron
Cover Photograph by Chris Clinton
Written by Michele Promaulayko, Riann Smith,
Jennifer Benjamin, Meaghan Buchan
Additional Text by Christie Griffin
Editor-in-Chief Joanna Coles

ISBN 978-1-61837-092-1

Distributed in Canada by Sterling Publishing
c/o Canadian Manda Group, 165 Dufferin Street
Toronto, Ontario, Canada M6K 3H6

Distributed in the United Kingdom by GMC Distribution Services
Castle Place, 166 High Street, Lewes, East Sussex, England BN7 1XU

Distributed in Australia by Capricorn Link (Australia) Pty. Ltd.
P.O. Box 704, Windsor, NSW 2756, Australia

For information about custom editions, special sales, and premium and corporate purchases, please contact Sterling Special Sales at 800-805-5489 or specialsales@sterlingpublishing.com.

Manufactured in China

2 4 6 8 10 9 7 5 3 1

www.sterlingpublishing.com